Hush!

Written by Liz Miles

Illustrated by Elif Balta Parks

Collins

Mum chops the logs.

Bang!

3

Josh has a den.

A duck runs in!

Chicks run in.

9

A big thing thuds.

Josh runs.

Josh has a posh den.

Hush!

/ch/

14

/qu/

🐾 Review: After reading 🐾

Use your assessment from hearing the children read to choose any GPCs, words or tricky words that need additional practice.

Read 1: Decoding

- Ask the children to tell you which of these words have a /sh/ sound.
  chops ship duck sink posh fish shock (*ship, posh, fish, shock*)
- Look at the "I spy sounds" pages (14–15) together. Discuss the picture with the children. Can they find items/examples of words that use the /ch/ and /qu/ sounds? (e.g. *torch, chimpanzee, chest, chair, bench, quilt, quack, quiet*)

Read 2: Prosody

- Model reading each page with expression to the children. After you have read each page, ask the children to have a go at reading with expression.
- On pages 2, 3, 6, 7 and 9, show the children how you read the sound effects and speech bubbles with expression, using greater emphasis for words with exclamation marks.

Read 3: Comprehension

- For every question ask the children how they know the answer. Ask:
  - What is Josh trying to do throughout the story? (*read his book quietly*)
  - How do the ducks and chicks make Josh feel and why? (e.g. *Josh is annoyed because the ducks and chicks are noisy and he wants it to be quiet so he can read his book.*)
  - What was Josh's mum making? (*a special den/a treehouse/somewhere for Josh to read*)
  - What does Josh think of his new den and how do you know? (e.g. *he is really pleased because he is smiling*)
  - Where do you like reading best? (e.g. *in the library, in my bedroom, in the reading corner, in the garden*)